Contents

About the story

The original title for this book was *Animal Farm: A Fairy Story*. In it, George Orwell described how a revolution against injustice could take place. He showed how it could be betrayed, then all it stood for be destroyed by its leaders. The story of *Animal Farm* follows the events of the Russian Revolution of 1917. However, Orwell wanted it to show a wider picture of how ordinary people could be lied to and taken advantage of by their corrupt leaders.

Some of the characters in the story are meant to represent real people in Russian history. Napoleon is Joseph Stalin, Snowball is Leon Trotsky, and Boxer represents the peasants who worked hard and fought to defend what they thought was a better life than they had had before. Foxwood Farm represents Great Britain, and Pinchfield Farm is Germany. Some of the events in the story mirror what happened in Russia. These are described at various points in this book.

About the author

George Orwell (whose real name was Eric Blair) was born in India in 1903. His father was a civil servant there, but his wife returned to England in 1904 with George and his older sister. George was educated at a preparatory school and then at Eton College. In 1922, after failing to get into university, he went to Burma (now Myanmar), where he served in the police force for five years.

When he returned to England, he travelled and lived among the poorest people in the country while writing and teaching. In the 1930s, he went to fight on the Communist side in the Spanish Civil War, where he was shot and wounded. It was his time in Spain that made him turn against Communism. *Animal Farm*, which was published in 1945, describes what he saw as the betrayal of the Russian Revolution by its leaders.

Towards the end of his life, Orwell lived on the Scottish island of Jura with his second wife. One of his other most famous books, *Nineteen Eighty-Four*, was published shortly before he died, in January 1950.

Cast of characters

Mr Jones
The drunken owner of
Manor Farm

Major
An old pig who has a
vision of the future

Snowball
An intelligent pig
and a rival of
Napoleon

Napoleon
A ruthless pig who
becomes leader of
Animal Farm

Squealer
A small, plump,
talkative pig

Boxer
A very strong, but
simple carthorse

Clover
A kind and caring
mare

Benjamin
A cynical donkey and
friend of Boxer

Mollie
A silly, vain horse

Muriel
A clever white goat

Minimus
A pig who writes poetry

Mr Pilkington
of Foxwood Farm

Mr Frederick
of Pinchfield Farm

Mr Whymper
A solicitor

Local farmers

Bluebell and Jessica
Farm dogs

Moses
Mr Jones's tame raven

1	Old Major tells the animals to prepare for a rebellion against humans. He gives them a set of rules and a song to sing about a land without human beings.

Mr Jones, of the Manor Farm, had locked the hen-houses for the night, but was too drunk to remember to shut the **pop-holes**. He lurched across the yard, kicking off his boots at the back door, drew himself a last glass of beer and made his way up to bed, where Mrs Jones was already snoring.

As soon as the light in the bedroom went out there was a stirring and a fluttering all through the farm buildings. Word had gone round that old Major had had a strange dream and wished to communicate it to the other animals.

---

pop-holes – small doors for the hens

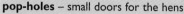

- What is your first impression of Mr Jones? How good a farmer do you think he is?

It had been agreed that they should all meet in the big barn as soon as Mr Jones was safely out of the way.

Old Major was so highly regarded that everyone was quite ready to lose an hour's sleep in order to hear what he had to say.

At one end of the big barn, on a sort of raised platform, Major was on his bed of straw, under a lantern which hung from a beam.

All the animals were now present except Moses. Major cleared his throat and began.

Comrades, I will come to the dream later. I have something else to say first.

I do not think, comrades, that I shall be with you for many months longer, and before I die I feel it my duty to pass on to you such wisdom as I have acquired.

I have had a long life, I have had much time for thought, and I think I may say that I understand the nature of life on this earth as well as any animal now living.

It is about this that I wish to speak to you.

'Now, comrades, what is the nature of this life of ours? Let us face it: our lives are miserable, **laborious** and short. We are born, we are given just so much food as will keep the breath in our bodies, and those of us who are capable of it are forced to work to the last atom of our strength; and the very instant that our usefulness has come to an end we are slaughtered with hideous cruelty. No animal in England knows the meaning of happiness or leisure after he is a year old. No animal in England is free. The life of an animal is misery and slavery: that is the plain truth.

hardworking

'But is this simply part of the order of nature? Is it because this land of ours is so poor that it cannot afford a decent life to those who dwell upon it? No, comrades, a thousand times no! The soil of England is fertile, its climate is good, it is capable of affording food in abundance to an enormously greater number of animals than now inhabit it. This single farm of ours would support a dozen horses, twenty cows, hundreds of sheep – and all of them living in a comfort and dignity that are now almost beyond our imagining. Why then do we continue in this miserable condition? Because nearly the whole of our produce is stolen from us by human beings. There, comrades, is the answer to all our problems. It is summed up in a single word – Man. Man is the only real enemy we have. Remove Man from the scene, and the root cause of hunger and overwork is abolished for ever.

'Man is the only creature that consumes without producing. He does not give milk, he does not lay eggs, he is too weak to pull the plough, he cannot run fast enough to catch rabbits. Yet he is lord of all the animals. He sets them to work, he gives back to them the bare minimum that will prevent them from starving, and the rest he keeps for himself. Our labour tills the soil, our dung fertilises it, and yet there is not one of us that owns more than his bare skin. You cows that I see before me, how many thousands of gallons of milk have you given during this past year? And what has happened to that milk which should have been breeding up sturdy calves? Every drop of it has gone down the throats of our enemies. And you hens, how many eggs have you laid this year, and how many of those eggs ever hatched into chickens? The rest have all gone to market to bring in money for Jones and his men. And you, Clover, where are those four foals you bore, who should have been the support and pleasure of your

4

old age? Each was sold at a year old – you will never see one of them again. In return for your four confinements and all your labour in the field, what have you ever had except your bare rations and a stall?

'And even the miserable lives we lead are not allowed to reach their natural span. For myself I do not grumble, for I am one of the lucky ones. I am twelve years old and have had over four hundred children. Such is the natural life of a pig. But no animal escapes the cruel knife in the end. You young porkers who are sitting in front of me, every one of you will scream your lives out at the block within a year. To that horror we all must come – cows, pigs, hens, sheep, everyone. You, Boxer, the very day that those great muscles of yours lose their power, Jones will sell you to the **knacker**, who will cut your throat and boil you down for the fox-hounds. As for the dogs, when they grow old and toothless, Jones ties a brick round their necks and drowns them in the nearest pond.'

someone who buys horses to kill

 Think About It

1 Why has Major chosen this time in his life to talk to the rest of the animals?

2 Why do you think Moses is not at the meeting?

3 What is your reaction to what Major says about how animals are treated? Would Major have thought differently if Jones had been a better, kinder farmer?

4 Major says that he will share his dream with the others. Can you think of other figures or prophets who have done this?

5 Major uses repetition and questions to make his message more powerful. Find examples of these techniques in this speech and look out for them in other speeches in the story.

The character of Major can be compared to Karl Marx (1818—1883). In 1847, Marx and Friedrich Engels published The Communist Manifesto *while they were living in* England. *This called for the workers to take control of 'the means of production' (things like factories, mines and transport systems) so that all profits could be shared out equally to everybody.*

All the evils of this life of ours spring from the tyranny of human beings.

Only get rid of Man, and the produce of our labour would be our own.

Almost overnight we could become rich and free.

What then must we do? Why, work night and day, body and soul, for the overthrow of the human race!

That is my message to you, comrades: Rebellion!

I do not know when that Rebellion will come, it might be in a week or in a hundred years, but I know that sooner or later justice will be done. Fix your eyes on that. And above all, pass on this message of mine to those who come after you.

Whatever goes upon two legs is an enemy. Whatever goes upon four legs, or has wings, is a friend. And remember also that in fighting against Man, we must not come to resemble him.

Even when you have conquered him, do not adopt his vices.

No animal must ever live in a house, or sleep in a bed, or wear clothes, or drink alcohol, or smoke tobacco, or touch money, or engage in trade. All the habits of Man are evil.

All animals are equal.

And above all, no animal must ever tyrannise over his own kind. Weak or strong, clever or simple, we are all brothers. No animal must ever kill any other animal.

- What are the nine things animals must not do?
- Which of Major's instructions do you think is the most important?
- Is Major saying that animals are Man's equals or superiors? Why?

And now, comrades, I will tell you about my dream.

It was a dream of the earth as it will be when Man has vanished.

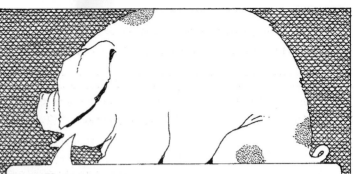

When I was a little pig, my mother used to sing an old song. It came back to me in my dream. I will sing you that song now, but when I have taught you the tune you can sing it better for yourselves. It is called 'Beasts of England'.

Beasts of England, beasts of Ireland,
Beasts of every land and **clime**,
Hearken to my joyful tidings
Of the golden future time.

Soon or late the day is coming,
Tyrant Man shall be o'erthrown,
And the fruitful fields of England
Shall be trod by beasts alone.

Rings shall vanish from our noses,
And the harness from our back,
Bit and spur shall rust forever,
Cruel whips no more will crack.

For that day we all must labour,
Though we die before it break;
Cows and horses, geese and turkeys,
All must toil for freedom's sake.

The song threw the animals into the wildest excitement. They were so delighted that they sang it right through five times. Unfortunately the uproar awoke Mr Jones, who sprang out of bed, sure there was a fox in the yard.

He seized the gun in his bedroom and let fly a shot into the darkness. The meeting broke up hurriedly. Everyone fled to his own sleeping-place. The whole farm was asleep in a moment.

clime – climate
Hearken – listen

● Find the words to other 'revolutionary songs' like 'The Marseillaise' and 'The Red Flag'. What do they have in common with 'Beasts of England'?

2	The animals rebel and drive Jones from the farm. Major's rules are written on the barn wall as the Seven Commandments.

Three nights later old Major died peacefully in his sleep. His body was buried at the foot of the orchard. This was early in March.

During the next three months there was much secret activity. The more intelligent animals did not know when the Rebellion would take place, but they saw clearly that it was their duty to prepare for it.

The work of teaching and organising the others fell upon the pigs, who were recognised as being the cleverest of the animals.

Pre-eminent among the pigs were two young **boars**, Snowball and Napoleon.

All the other male pigs were **porkers**. The best known was Squealer. He was a brilliant talker.

Napoleon was rather fierce-looking, not much of a talker but with a reputation for getting his own way.

Snowball was quicker in speech and more inventive.

The others said of Squealer that he could turn black into white.

Pre-eminent – most important
boars – male pigs kept for breeding
porkers – pigs raised for meat

• Which of the pigs do you think will be most influential in the Rebellion? Why?

These three had **elaborated** old Major's teachings into a complete system of thought, to which they gave the name of Animalism. They held secret meetings in the barn.

At the beginning they met with much stupidity and **apathy**.

Will there still be sugar after the Rebellion, and ribbons?

Comrade, ribbons are the badge of slavery.

Mollie did not sound very convinced.

The pigs had an even harder struggle to counteract the lies put about by Moses, who was also a clever talker. He claimed to know of a mysterious country called Sugarcandy Mountain, to which all animals went when they died.

Boxer and Clover had great difficulty in thinking for themselves, but they absorbed everything that they were told.

The animals hated Moses because he told tales and did no work, but some of them believed in Sugarcandy Mountain.

elaborated – added detail to
apathy – lack of interest

Now, as it turned out, the Rebellion was achieved much earlier and more easily than anyone had expected.

Mr Jones had taken to drinking more than was good for him. His men were idle and dishonest, the fields were full of weeds and the animals were underfed.

On **Midsummer's Eve**, which was a Saturday, Mr Jones got so drunk at the Red Lion that he did not come home till Sunday.

The men had milked the cows and then gone **rabbiting** without bothering to feed the animals.

When Mr Jones got back he went to sleep, so that when evening came the animals were still unfed.

At last they could stand it no longer. One of the cows broke in the door of the store-shed and the animals began to help themselves.

It was just then that Mr Jones woke up.

Midsummer's Eve – 23 June
rabbiting – rabbit-hunting

The next moment he and his men were in the store-shed with whips in their hands, lashing out in all directions.

This was more than the hungry animals could bear. Though nothing of the kind had been planned they flung themselves on their tormentors.

After only a moment or two they gave up trying to defend themselves. A minute later all five were in full flight.

And so, almost before they knew what was happening, the Rebellion had been successfully carried through: Manor Farm was theirs.

For the first few minutes the animals could hardly believe in their good fortune. Their first act was to gallop in a body right round the boundaries of the farm, as though to make quite sure that no human being was hiding anywhere upon it; then they raced back to the farm buildings to wipe out the last traces of Jones's hated reign. The harness-room at the end of the stables was broken open; the bits, the nose-rings, the dog-chains, the cruel knives with which Mr Jones had been used to castrate the pigs and lambs, were all flung down the well. The reins, the halters, the blinkers, the **degrading** nosebags, were thrown on to the rubbish fire which was burning in the yard. So were the whips. All the animals **capered** with joy when they saw the whips going up in flames. Snowball also threw on to the fire the ribbons with which the horses' manes and tails had usually been decorated on market days.

insulting

danced

'Ribbons,' he said, 'should be considered as clothes, which are the mark of a human being. All animals should go naked.'

When Boxer heard this he fetched the small straw hat which he wore in summer to keep the flies out of his ears, and flung it on the fire with the rest.

In a very little while the animals had destroyed everything that reminded them of Mr Jones. Napoleon then led them back to the store-shed and served out a double ration of corn to everybody, with two biscuits for each dog. Then they sang 'Beasts of England' from end to end seven times running, and after that they settled down for the night and slept as they had never slept before.

But they woke at dawn as usual, and suddenly remembering the glorious thing that had happened they all raced out into the pasture together. A little way down the pasture there was a **knoll** that commanded a view of most of the farm. The animals rushed to the top of it and gazed round them in the clear morning light. Yes, it was theirs – everything that they could see was theirs! In the ecstasy of that thought they **gambolled** round and round, they hurled themselves into the air in great leaps of excitement. They rolled in the dew, they cropped mouthfuls of the sweet summer grass, they kicked up clods of the black earth and snuffed its rich scent. Then they made a tour of inspection of the whole farm and surveyed with speechless admiration the ploughland, the hayfield, the orchard, the pool, the spinney. It was as though they had never seen these things before, and even now they could hardly believe that it was all their own.

small hill or mound

danced and jumped

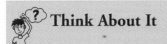

Think About It

1 In what way is the Rebellion accidental?

2 Could Jones have done anything differently to prevent the Rebellion?

3 Moses is said to represent the church in Russia, see page 10. Can you think why?

4 Why are Boxer and Clover important to the success of the Rebellion?

5 Should Boxer have thrown his straw hat on the fire to burn with the ribbons?

6 Why do the animals now look at the farm 'as though they had never seen these things before'?

In the early stages of the Russian Revolution, the Tzar and his troops attacked rebel workers with great ferocity, just as Jones attacks the animals.

They halted in silence outside the farmhouse. That was theirs too, but they were frightened to go inside. After a moment, however, Snowball and Napoleon butted the door open.

They tiptoed from room to room, gazing with awe at the unbelievable luxury.

Some hams hanging in the kitchen were taken out for burial, and the barrel of beer in the **scullery** was **stove in**, otherwise nothing was touched. All agreed that no animal must ever live there.

Comrades, we have a long day before us. Today we begin the hay harvest.

But there is another matter that must be attended to first.

The pigs now revealed that they had taught themselves to read and write from an old spelling book. Napoleon sent for pots of paint. Snowball painted out MANOR FARM from the gate and in its place painted ANIMAL FARM. After this they went back to the big barn.

Snowball and Napoleon explained that the pigs had succeeded in reducing the principles of Animalism to Seven Commandments.

scullery – kitchen room used for cold storage
stove in – broken open

- Why were the hams buried? Does this make us admire the animals, or find them amusing?
- Why would the animals 'tiptoe' round the farmhouse?
- Russia became the 'Soviet Union' after the Revolution, and other countries have changed their name after revolutions or gaining independence. Why might this be important?

These Commandments would form an unalterable law by which all the animals must live for ever. The Commandments were written on the wall in great white letters.

THE SEVEN COMMANDMENTS

1. Whatever goes upon two legs is an enemy.
2. Whatever goes upon four legs, or has wings, is a freind.
3. No animal shall wear clothes.
4. No animal shall sleep in a bed.
5. No animal shall drink alcohol.
6. No animal shall kill any other animal.
7. All animals are equal.

At this moment the cows set up a loud lowing. They had not been milked for twenty-four hours.

The pigs sent for buckets and milked the cows fairly successfully. Soon there were five buckets of creamy milk.

What is going to happen to all that milk?

Never mind the milk, comrades. That will be attended to. The harvest is more important. Comrade Snowball will lead the way. I shall follow in a few minutes. Forward, comrades!

So the animals trooped down to the hayfield to begin the harvest ...

... and when they came back in the evening it was noticed that the milk had disappeared.

 • What do you think happened to the milk?

3	The first harvest is gathered in. Education classes begin and Napoleon and Snowball start to quarrel.

How they toiled and sweated! But their efforts were rewarded for the harvest was an even bigger success than they had hoped for. It was a drawback that no animal was able to use any tool that involved standing on his hind legs.

The pigs did not actually work but directed and supervised the others. With their superior knowledge it was natural that they should assume the leadership.

Gee up, comrade.

All through that summer the work of the farm went like clockwork. The animals were happy. There was more leisure too.

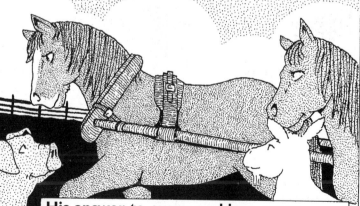

Boxer was the admiration of everybody. He seemed like three horses in one; there were days when the entire work of the farm seemed to rest upon his mighty shoulders. From morning to night he was always at the spot where the work was hardest.

His answer to every problem, every setback, was 'I will work harder!' – which he had adopted as his personal motto.

- Is 'directing' and 'supervising' the same as actually 'working'?
- Do you think all the animals have Boxer's attitude to work on the farm, or is he different?

Nobody stole, nobody grumbled. Nobody **shirked** – or almost nobody.

Mollie, it was true, was not good at getting up in the mornings. And when there was work to be done the cat could never be found. Old Benjamin did his work in the same slow obstinate way.

On Sundays there was no work. After breakfast there was a ceremony. First came the hoisting of the flag. Snowball had found an old green tablecloth and painted on it a hoof and horn in white.

After the hoisting of the flag all the animals trooped into the big barn for the Meeting.

Here the work was planned out and **resolutions** were put forward and debated.

It was always the pigs who put forward the resolutions.

The other animals understood how to vote, but could never think of any resolutions of their own.

Snowball and Napoleon were by far the most active in the debates. But it was noticed that these two were never in agreement.

The Meeting always ended with the singing of 'Beasts of England'.

shirked – avoided work
resolutions – plans/schemes

- Why does Snowball think Animal Farm needs a flag?
- What do the horn and hoof and the colour of the flag represent?

The pigs had set aside the harness-room as a headquarters for themselves. Here, in the evenings, they studied blacksmithing, carpentering and other necessary arts from books from the farmhouse.

Snowball also busied himself with organising Animal Committees.

Egg Production Committee

Clean Tails League

Whiter Wool Movement

On the whole these were a failure.

The reading and writing classes, however, were a great success.

The pigs could already read and write.

The dogs could read fairly well.

Muriel could read better than the dogs ...

... and Benjamin could read as well as any pig.

Boxer could not get past the letter D.

Mollie refused to learn any but the letters which spelt her own name.

None of the other animals could get further than the letter A. It was also found that the stupider animals such as the sheep, hens and ducks, were unable to learn the Seven commandments by heart. Snowball declared that the Commandments could be reduced to a single **maxim**.

FOUR LEGS GOOD, TWO LEGS BAD was inscribed on the barn.

Four legs good, two legs bad. Four legs good, two legs bad.

The sheep developed a great liking for it.

maxim – rule

Napoleon took no interest in Snowball's committees. He said that the education of the young was more important than anything that could be done for those who were already grown up. It happened that Jessie and Bluebell had both **whelped** soon after the hay harvest, giving birth between them to nine sturdy puppies. As soon as they were **weaned**, Napoleon took them away from their mothers, saying that he would make himself responsible for their education. He took them up into a loft which could only be reached by a ladder from the harness-room, and there kept them in such **seclusion** that the rest of the farm soon forgot their existence.

given birth

able to survive without mother's milk

isolation

The mystery of where the milk went to was soon cleared up. It was mixed every day into the pigs' mash. The early apples were now ripening, and the grass of the orchard was littered with windfalls. The animals had assumed as a matter of course that these would be shared out equally; one day, however, the order went forth that all the windfalls were to be collected and brought to the harness-room for the use of the pigs. At this some of the other animals murmured, but it was no use. All the pigs were in full agreement on this point, even Snowball and Napoleon. Squealer was sent to make the necessary explanations to the others.

'Comrades!' he cried. 'You do not imagine, I hope, that we pigs are doing this in a spirit of selfishness and privilege? Many of us actually dislike milk and apples. I dislike them myself. Our sole object in taking these things is to preserve our health. Milk and apples (this has been proved by Science, comrades) contain substances absolutely necessary to the well-being of a pig. We pigs are brain-workers. The whole management and organisation of this farm depend on us. Day and night we are watching over your welfare. It is for *your* sake that we drink that milk and eat those apples. Do you know what would happen if we pigs failed in our duty? Jones would come back! Yes, Jones would come back! Surely, comrades,' cried Squealer almost pleadingly, skipping from side to side and whisking his tail, 'surely there is no one among you who wants to see Jones come back?'

Now if there was one thing that the animals were completely certain of, it was that they did not want Jones back. When it was put to them in this light, they had no more to say. The importance of keeping the pigs in good health was all too obvious. So it was agreed without further argument that the milk and the windfall apples (and also the main crop of apples when they ripened) should be reserved for the pigs alone.

 Think About It

1 Why do you think the Animal Committees were not successful?

2 Does the slogan 'Four legs good, two legs bad' accurately summarise all the Commandments? Do you think Major would have approved of it?

3 Orwell said that the turning point in the story was when the pigs decided to keep all the milk and apples for themselves. If this is true, what might be starting to happen on Animal Farm?

4 Why might Napoleon have taken the puppies to train?

5 Nowadays, Squealer would be called a 'spin doctor'. Do you think his explanation as to why the pigs need the milk is reasonable?

6 Look again at Major's speech on pages 4–5. Does Squealer use any similar techniques?

4	Jones and his men try to recapture the farm.

By the late summer the news of Animal Farm had spread across half the country. Snowball and Napoleon sent out pigeons to neighbouring farms.

Most of this time Mr Jones had spent in the Red Lion complaining. The other farmers sympathised but did not give him much help.

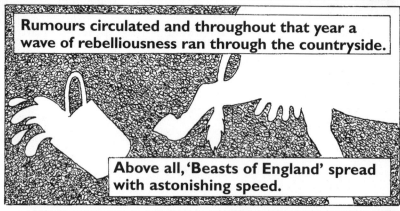

They were frightened by the rebellion on Animal Farm and anxious to prevent their own animals from learning too much about it. They put it about that the animals were rapidly starving to death.

Rumours circulated and throughout that year a wave of rebelliousness ran through the countryside.

Above all, 'Beasts of England' spread with astonishing speed.

When the human beings listened to it, they trembled, hearing in it a **prophecy** of their future doom.

Early in October, when the corn was cut, pigeons came whirling through the air in the wildest excitement. Jones and all his men with others from Foxwood and Pinchfield were coming.

prophecy – prediction of the future

• Why are the other farms (Foxwood/Britain and Pinchfield/Germany) reluctant to give Jones any help?

They were all carrying sticks except Jones who was marching ahead with a gun.

Obviously they were going to attempt the recapture of the farm.

This had long been expected, and all preparations had been made.

Snowball gave his orders quickly, and in a couple of minutes every animal was at his post.

As the human beings approached, Snowball launched his first attack.

Pigeons dropped their dung on them while geese pecked viciously at their legs.

Muriel, Benjamin and all the sheep with Snowball at the head of them rushed forward and prodded and butted the men.

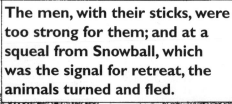

The men, with their sticks, were too strong for them; and at a squeal from Snowball, which was the signal for retreat, the animals turned and fled.

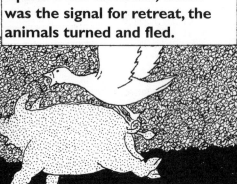

The men gave a shout of triumph and rushed after them.

This was just what Snowball had intended. As soon as they were inside the yard, the horses, cows and the rest of the pigs emerged in their rear, cutting them off.

Snowball now gave the signal for the charge.

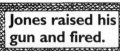

Jones raised his gun and fired.

The **pellets** scored bloody streaks along Snowball's back, and a sheep dropped dead.

Jones was hurled into a pile of dung and his gun flew out of his hands.

---

pellets – shotgun pellets

- Snowball not only plans the defence of Animal Farm but actually leads it. What does this show about his style of leadership?

They were all carrying sticks except Jones who was marching ahead with a gun.

Obviously they were going to attempt the recapture of the farm.

This had long been expected, and all preparations had been made.

Snowball gave his orders quickly, and in a couple of minutes every animal was at his post.

As the human beings approached, Snowball launched his first attack.

Pigeons dropped their dung on them while geese pecked viciously at their legs.

Muriel, Benjamin and all the sheep with Snowball at the head of them rushed forward and prodded and butted the men.

The men, with their sticks, were too strong for them; and at a squeal from Snowball, which was the signal for retreat, the animals turned and fled.

The men gave a shout of triumph and rushed after them.

This was just what Snowball had intended. As soon as they were inside the yard, the horses, cows and the rest of the pigs emerged in their rear, cutting them off.

Snowball now gave the signal for the charge.

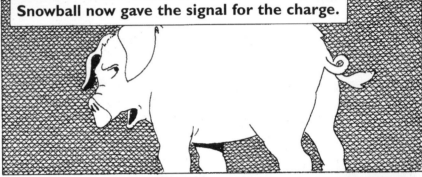

Jones raised his gun and fired.

The **pellets** scored bloody streaks along Snowball's back, and a sheep dropped dead.

Jones was hurled into a pile of dung and his gun flew out of his hands.

pellets – shotgun pellets

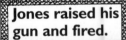
• Snowball not only plans the defence of Animal Farm but actually leads it. What does this show about his style of leadership?

The most terrifying was Boxer, rearing up and striking out with his great hoofs.

His very first blow took a **stable-lad** from Foxwood on the skull.

At the sight, several men dropped their sticks and tried to run. Panic overtook them.

There was not an animal that did not take **vengeance** on them.

Within five minutes of their invasion, they were in retreat.

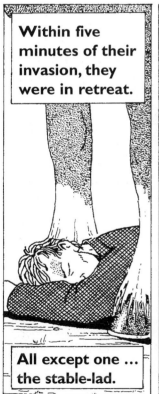

All except one ... the stable-lad.

He is dead. I have no wish to take life, not even human life.

Where's Mollie?

Mollie was missing. It was feared that the men might have harmed her, or carried her off. However, she was found hiding in her stall.

When the others came back from looking for her, it was to find that the stable-lad, who in fact was only stunned, had recovered and made off.

stable-lad – farm worker who looks after horses
vengeance – revenge

 • How surprised are you at Mollie's cowardice?

The animals now reassembled in the wildest excitement.

An **impromptu** celebration of the victory was held immediately.

The flag was run up and 'Beasts of England' was sung a number of times.

The sheep was given a solemn funeral.

Snowball made a little speech, emphasising the need for all animals to be ready to die for Animal Farm if need be.

A military decoration, 'Animal Hero, First Class', was conferred on Snowball and Boxer.

'Animal hero, Second Class', was conferred on the dead sheep.

There was much discussion as to what the battle should be called. In the end it was named the Battle of the Cowshed. Mr Jones's gun had been found. It was decided to set the gun up at the foot of the flagstaff and to fire it on October the twelfth, the anniversary of the Battle and on Midsummer Day, the anniversary of the Rebellion.

impromptu – unplanned

5	Snowball produces plans to build a windmill but is driven from the farm by Napoleon and his dogs.

As winter drew on Mollie became more and more troublesome. She was late for work and complained of mysterious pains. She would go to the pool where she would stand gazing at her own reflection in the water. But there were rumours of something more serious.

Clover took her aside.

I saw one of Mr Pilkington's men talking to you.

It isn't true! It isn't true!

Three days later Mollie disappeared.

Pigeons reported that they had seen her between the shafts of a smart **dog-cart**. She appeared to be enjoying herself.

None of the animals ever mentioned Mollie again.

In January there came bitterly hard weather and nothing could be done in the fields. Many meetings were held in the big barn. It had come to be accepted that the pigs should decide policy, though their decisions had to be **ratified** by a majority vote.

Snowball and Napoleon disagreed at every point.

Each had his own following.

dog-cart – small, two-wheeled carriage
ratified – confirmed

Snowball was full of plans for **innovations** and improvements. Napoleon produced no schemes of his own, but said that Snowball's would come to nothing, and seemed to be biding his time.

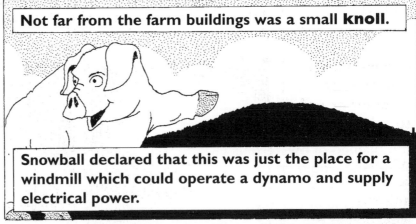

Not far from the farm buildings was a small **knoll**.

Snowball declared that this was just the place for a windmill which could operate a dynamo and supply electrical power.

Within a few weeks Snowball's plans for the windmill were worked out.

Snowball used a shed which had a smooth floor, suitable for drawing on.

The other animals came to look at Snowball's drawings at least once a day. Napoleon arrived unexpectedly. He looked closely at every detail, then lifted his leg and urinated over the plans and walked out without uttering a word.

The whole farm was deeply divided on the subject of the windmill.

Snowball maintained it could be done in a year.

Napoleon argued that if they wasted time on the windmill they would all starve to death.

Benjamin refused to believe either.

He said life would go on as it had always gone on – that is, badly.

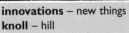

innovations – new things
knoll – hill

At last Snowball's plans were completed. At the Meeting whether or not to begin work on the windmill was to be put to the vote. The animals assembled in the big barn.

Snowball set forth his reasons for building the windmill.

Napoleon said that the windmill was nonsense and sat down again.

He had spoken for barely thirty seconds.

Snowball broke into a passionate appeal in favour of the windmill.

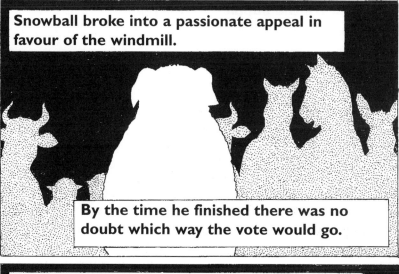

By the time he finished there was no doubt which way the vote would go.

Napoleon stood up and uttered a high-pitched whimper.

Nine enormous dogs came bounding into the barn. They dashed straight for Snowball.

In a moment he was out of the door and they were after him.

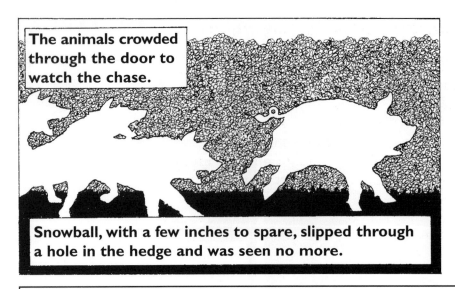

The animals crowded through the door to watch the chase.

Snowball, with a few inches to spare, slipped through a hole in the hedge and was seen no more.

Silent and terrified, the animals crept back into the barn. In a moment the dogs came bounding back. They were the puppies Napoleon had reared. It was noticed that they wagged their tails to him in the same way as the other dogs used to do to Mr Jones.

Napoleon, with the dogs following him, now mounted on to the raised portion of the floor where Major had previously stood to deliver his speech. He announced that from now on the Sunday morning Meetings would come to an end. They were unnecessary, he said, and wasted time. In future all questions relating to the working of the farm would be settled by a special committee of pigs, **presided over** by himself. These would meet in private and afterwards communicate their decisions to the others. The animals would still assemble on Sunday mornings to salute the flag, sing 'Beasts of England' and receive their orders for the week; but there would be no more debates.

in charge of

In spite of the shock that Snowball's expulsion had given them, the animals were dismayed by this announcement. Several of them would have protested if they could have found the right arguments. Even Boxer was vaguely troubled. He set his ears back, shook his forelock several times and tried hard to marshal his thoughts; but in the end he could not think of anything to say. Some of the pigs themselves, however, were more **articulate**. Four young porkers in the front row uttered shrill squeals of disapproval, and all four of them sprang to their feet and began speaking at once. But suddenly the dogs sitting round Napoleon let out deep, menacing growls, and the pigs fell silent and sat down again. Then the sheep broke out into a tremendous bleating of 'Four legs good, two legs bad!' which went on for nearly a quarter of an hour and put an end to any chance of discussion.

able to speak well

Afterwards Squealer was sent round the farm to explain the new arrangements to the others.

'Comrades,' he said, 'I trust that every animal here appreciates the sacrifice that Comrade Napoleon has made in taking this extra labour upon himself. Do not imagine, comrades, that leadership is a pleasure! On the contrary, it is a deep and heavy responsibility. Nobody believes more firmly than Comrade Napoleon that all animals are equal. He would be only too happy to let you make your decisions for yourselves. But sometimes you might make the wrong decisions, comrades, and then where should we be? Suppose you had decided to follow Snowball, with his moonshine of windmills – Snowball, who, as we now know, was no better than a criminal?'

'He fought bravely at the Battle of the Cowshed,' said somebody.

'Bravery is not enough,' said Squealer. 'Loyalty and obedience are more important. And as to the Battle of the Cowshed, I believe the time will come when we shall find that Snowball's part in it was much exaggerated. Discipline, comrades, iron discipline! That is the watchword for today. One false step, and our enemies would be upon us. Surely, comrades, you do not want Jones back?'

 Think About It

1 Mollie represents those Russians who did not support the Revolution because it threatened their own interests. Do you have any sympathy with what Mollie does?

2 Look again at page 28 and Snowball's and Napoleon's arguments about the windmill. Would you have been for or against building it?

3 Benjamin does not believe that his life will ever change – no matter what happens. Is he right?

4 If Napoleon took the puppies just after they were born, does this mean he always planned to seize power?

5 If 'all animals are equal', why are the dogs being controlled by Napoleon?

6 Why is Squealer the one who always explains changes to the other animals? (Look back at page 9.)

Leon Trotsky was one of the early leaders of the Russian Revolution. He organised the Red Army but quarrelled with Stalin. In 1927 he was exiled from Russia, and later assassinated while living in Mexico.

Once again this argument was unanswerable. Boxer voiced the general feeling.

If Comrade Napoleon says it, it must be right.

From then on he adopted the maxim, 'Napoleon is always right,' in addition to 'I will work harder.'

Every Sunday morning the animals assembled to receive their orders.

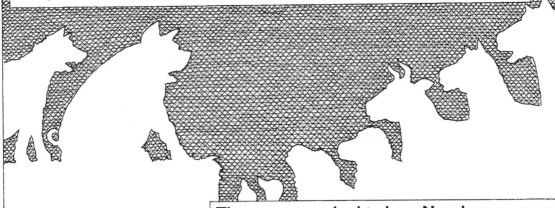

They were surprised to hear Napoleon announce that the windmill was to be built after all.

He warned the animals that this would mean very hard work; it might even be necessary to reduce their rations.

Squealer explained that the plan had actually been stolen from among Napoleon's papers. Napoleon had seemed to oppose the windmill to get rid of Snowball, who was a dangerous character and a bad influence.

- Has Boxer thought at all about his new 'maxim'?
- If Snowball has gone for good, why does Napoleon feel it necessary to blacken his name?

6	The pigs begin to make a few changes and the windmill is destroyed in a storm.

All that year the animals worked like slaves. But they were happy, aware that everything they did was for the benefit of themselves.

They worked a sixty-hour week, and in August Napoleon announced there would be work on Sunday afternoons as well.

This work was strictly voluntary, but any animal who absented himself from it would have his **rations** reduced by half.

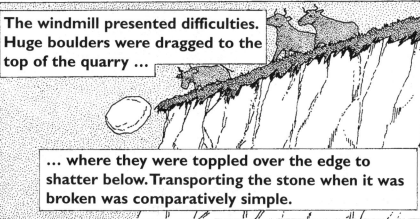

The windmill presented difficulties. Huge boulders were dragged to the top of the quarry …

… where they were toppled over the edge to shatter below. Transporting the stone when it was broken was comparatively simple.

Nothing could have been achieved without Boxer.

Clover warned him not to overstrain himself.

In his spare moments, of which there were not many, he would go alone to collect a load of broken stone and drag it down to the site of the windmill.

---

rations – a daily food allowance

 • Look back at page 17. How has life on the farm changed for the animals?

As the summer wore on, unforeseen shortages began to make themselves felt. There was need of **paraffin oil**, nails, string, dog biscuits and iron for the horses' hoofs, none of which could be produced on the farm.

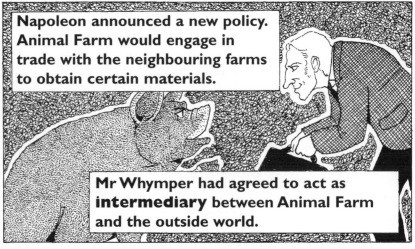

Napoleon announced a new policy. Animal Farm would engage in trade with the neighbouring farms to obtain certain materials.

Mr Whymper had agreed to act as **intermediary** between Animal Farm and the outside world.

Once again the animals were conscious of a vague unease.

Squealer assured them that the resolution against trade and using money had never been passed, or even suggested.

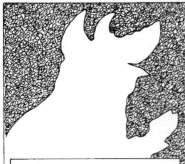

It was pure imagination, probably traceable in the beginning to lies circulated by Snowball.

A few animals still felt faintly doubtful.

Are you certain that this is not something that you have dreamed, comrades? Have you any record of such a resolution? Is it written down anywhere?

Every Monday Mr Whymper visited. There was as yet no contact between Animal Farm and the outside world, but there were rumours that Napoleon was about to enter into a business arrangement either with Mr Pilkington or Mr Frederick.

paraffin oil – for lamps
intermediary – go-between

 • Which of Major's instructions is being ignored now?

It was about this time that the pigs suddenly moved into the farmhouse. Squealer said that the pigs should have a quiet place to work in. It also suited the dignity of the Leader (for he had taken to speaking of Napoleon under the title of 'Leader') to live in a house more than a sty.

The animals were disturbed when they heard that the pigs slept in the beds.

Muriel, read me the Fourth Commandment. Does it not say something about never sleeping in a bed?

With some difficulty Muriel spelt it out.

It says, 'No animal shall sleep in a bed with sheets'.

Clover had not remembered that the Fourth Commandment mentioned sheets; but as it was there on the wall, it must have done so.

Squealer happened to be passing, attended by two or three dogs.

The rule was against sheets, which are a human invention. We have removed the sheets and sleep between blankets.

- When Napoleon begins to be called 'Leader', another of Major's instructions is being ignored. Which one?
- What has happened to the Fourth Commandment?

By the autumn the animals were tired but happy. They had had a hard year but the windmill was almost half built.

November came, with raging winds. There came a night when the gale was so violent the buildings rocked.

In the morning the animals came out of their stalls. A terrible sight met their eyes.

The windmill was in ruins.

They dashed down to the spot. Napoleon, who seldom moved out of a walk, raced ahead.

Snowball has done this! To avenge himself for his expulsion, this traitor has crept here under cover of night and destroyed our work.

Here and now I pronounce the death sentence upon Snowball. 'Animal Hero, Second Class', and half a **bushel** of apples to any animal who brings him to justice.

The animals were shocked.

The footprints of a pig were discovered. Napoleon pronounced them to be Snowball's.

No more delays, comrades! There is work to be done.

This very morning we begin rebuilding the windmill.

We will build all through the winter, rain or shine.

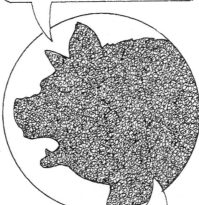

We will teach this miserable traitor that he cannot undo our work so easily.

There must be no alteration in our plans.

Forward, comrades! Long live the windmill! Long live Animal Farm!

bushel – a measurement of weight

It was a bitter winter. The animals carried on rebuilding the windmill, knowing the outside world was watching them. The human beings pretended not to believe Snowball had destroyed the windmill.

They said it had fallen down because the walls were too thin. The animals knew this was not the case. Still, it had been decided to build the walls three feet thick this time instead of eighteen inches.

In January food fell short. It would be necessary to **procure** more grain from somewhere.

Squealer announced that the hens must surrender their eggs.

Napoleon had accepted, through Whymper, a contract for four hundred eggs a week.

The hens raised a terrible outcry. They protested that to take their eggs now was murder.

There was something like a rebellion. The hens made a determined effort to **thwart** Napoleon's wishes. Their method was to fly up to the rafters and lay their eggs, which smashed on the floor. Napoleon ordered the hens' rations to be stopped.

For five days the hens held out. Nine died.

Whymper heard nothing of this, and the eggs were duly delivered.

procure – obtain, get
thwart – stop

 Who do you believe about the windmill: Napoleon or the human beings?

Early in the spring, an alarming thing was discovered. Snowball was secretly **frequenting** the farm by night! Every night, it was said, he came and performed all kinds of mischief. Whenever anything went wrong it became usual to **attribute it to** Snowball.

The cows declared that Snowball milked them in their sleep.

The rats were also said to be in league with Snowball.

Napoleon decreed that there should be a full investigation. He made a tour of inspection. He found traces of Snowball almost everywhere.

He has been here! I can smell him distinctly!

The animals were thoroughly frightened.

In the evening Squealer called them together.

Comrades! A most terrible thing has been discovered. Snowball has sold himself to Frederick of Pinchfield Farm, who is plotting to attack us.

Snowball was Jones's secret agent all the time.

Did we not see how he attempted to get us defeated and destroyed at the Battle of the Cowshed?

frequenting – visiting
attribute it to – blame on

The animals were stupefied. They thought they remembered Snowball at the Battle.

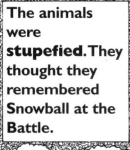

I do not believe that. Snowball fought bravely. I saw him myself.

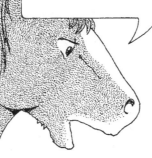

It is all written down in secret documents we have found.

In reality he was trying to lure us to our doom.

But he was wounded. We all saw him running with blood.

That was part of the arrangement. Jones's shot only grazed him.

I could show you this in his own writing, if you were able to read it.

Do you not remember how Snowball suddenly turned and fled? And that Comrade Napoleon sprang forward with a cry of 'Death to Humanity!' and sank his teeth in Jones's leg?

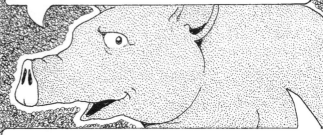

I do not believe that Snowball was a traitor at the beginning.

Our leader has stated **categorically** that Snowball was Jones's agent.

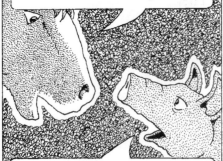

If Comrade Napoleon says it, it must be right.

That is the true spirit, comrade.

I warn every animal to keep his eyes open. We think that some of Snowball's secret agents are amongst us!

stupefied – amazed, shocked, speechless
categorically – without any doubt

> **Napoleon organises the public execution of any animal who has disagreed with him. There is no doubt now who is in charge of Animal Farm!**

Four days later, in the late afternoon, Napoleon ordered all the animals to assemble in the yard. When they were all gathered together, Napoleon emerged from the farmhouse, wearing both his medals (for he had recently awarded himself 'Animal Hero, First Class' and 'Animal Hero, Second Class'), with his nine huge dogs frisking round him and uttering growls that sent shivers down all the animals' spines. They all cowered silently in their places, seeming to know in advance that some terrible thing was about to happen.

Napoleon stood sternly surveying his audience; then he uttered a high-pitched whimper. Immediately the dogs bounded forward, seized four of the pigs by the ear and dragged them, squealing with pain and terror, to Napoleon's feet. The pigs' ears were bleeding, the dogs had tasted blood, and for a few moments they appeared to go quite mad. To the amazement of everybody, three of them flung themselves upon Boxer. Boxer saw them coming and put out his great hoof, caught a dog in mid-air and pinned him to the ground. The dog shrieked for mercy and the other two fled with their tails between their legs. Boxer looked at Napoleon to know whether he should crush the dog to death or let it go. Napoleon appeared to change **countenance**, and sharply ordered Boxer to let the dog go, whereat Boxer lifted his hoof, and the dog slunk away, bruised and howling.

Presently the **tumult** died down. The four pigs waited, trembling, with guilt written on every line of their countenances. Napoleon now called upon them to confess their crimes. They were the same four pigs as had protested when Napoleon abolished the Sunday Meetings. Without any further prompting they confessed that they had been secretly in touch with Snowball ever since his expulsion, that they had collaborated with him in destroying the windmill, and that they had entered into an agreement with him to hand over Animal Farm to Mr Frederick. They added that Snowball had privately admitted to them that he had been Jones's secret agent for years past. When they had finished their confession the dogs promptly tore their throats out, and in a terrible voice Napoleon demanded whether any other animal had anything to confess.

facial expression

noise/row

The three hens who had been the ringleaders in the attempted rebellion over the eggs now came forward and stated that Snowball had appeared to them in a dream and incited them to disobey Napoleon's orders. They, too, were slaughtered. Then a goose came forward and confessed to having **secreted** six ears of corn during the last year's harvest and eaten them in the night. Then a sheep confessed to having urinated in the drinking-pool – urged to do this, so she said, by Snowball – and two other sheep confessed to having murdered an old ram, an especially devoted follower of Napoleon, by chasing him round and round a bonfire when he was suffering from a cough. They were all slain on the spot. And so the tale of confessions and executions went on, until there was a pile of corpses lying before Napoleon's feet and the air was heavy with the smell of blood, which had been unknown there since the expulsion of Jones.

hidden

 Think About It

1 Napoleon crushes the hens' rebellion with great cruelty. Is he now any different from Jones?

2 Are the stories about Snowball secretly visiting the farm true, do you think? If not, why does Napoleon encourage them?

3 How does Squealer's account of the Battle of the Cowshed differ from what Boxer remembers?

4 How is Boxer persuaded to ignore the evidence of his own eyes?

5 What is threatening about what Squealer says at the end of page 40?

6 Is the dogs' attack on Boxer accidental?

7 Look at the confessions made by the animals. Are they all real and why do you think the animals are so willing to confess when they know that they will be put to death?

When it was all over, the remaining animals, except for the pigs and dogs, crept away. They were shaken and miserable. They made their way onto the little knoll.

I do not understand it. I would not have believed such things could happen on our farm.

Clover knew it was not for this that she and all the other animals had hoped and toiled. It was not for this that they had built the windmill and faced the pellets of Jones's gun.

She began to sing 'Beasts of England'. The other animals sang it, slowly and mournfully.

Squealer approached. He announced that 'Beasts of England' had been abolished.

From now onwards it was forbidden to sing it.

It is no longer needed. 'Beasts of England' was the song of the Rebellion. But the Rebellion is now completed.

The execution of the traitors was the final act.

So 'Beasts of England' was heard no more. In its place, Minimus had composed another song which began:
Animal Farm, Animal Farm, Never through me shalt thou come to harm!
and this was sung every Sunday morning. But somehow neither the words nor the tune seemed to the animals to come up to 'Beasts of England'.

* Remember the 'tyranny' of Jones's rule of the farm. What features of tyranny can you see there now?

A few days later, some of the animals remembered – or thought they remembered – the Sixth Commandment. Clover fetched Muriel.

6. No animal shall kill any other animal without cause.

7. All animals are equal.

The animals worked harder to rebuild the windmill.

On Sunday mornings Squealer would read out figures proving that the production of foodstuff had increased by two, three, or five hundred per cent.

The animals felt they would sooner have less figures and more food.

Napoleon was attended not only by his dogs but by a cockerel who acted as a kind of trumpeter before Napoleon spoke. It was announced that the gun would be fired on Napoleon's birthday, as well as on the other two anniversaries.

- What has happened to the Sixth Commandment?
- What does Squealer hope to achieve with his lists of figures?

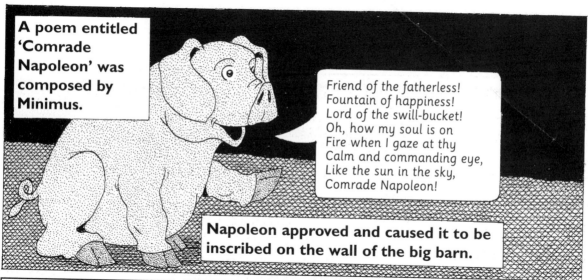

A poem entitled 'Comrade Napoleon' was composed by Minimus.

Friend of the fatherless!
Fountain of happiness!
Lord of the swill-bucket!
Oh, how my soul is on
Fire when I gaze at thy
Calm and commanding eye,
Like the sun in the sky,
Comrade Napoleon!

Napoleon approved and caused it to be inscribed on the wall of the big barn.

At the same time there were rumours that Frederick and his men were planning to attack and destroy the windmill. Snowball was known to be still skulking on Pinchfield Farm. Terrible stories were leaking out about the cruelties Frederick practised on his animals.

The animals clamoured to attack Pinchfield. But Squealer counselled them to avoid rash actions.

In autumn the windmill was finished.

Napoleon announced that the mill would be named Napoleon Mill.

Napoleon warned that Frederick and his men might attack at any moment.

The very next morning the attack came.

The animals **sallied forth** to meet them. There were fifteen men, with half a dozen guns between them, and they opened fire as soon as they got within fifty yards.

The animals were driven back. They took refuge in the farm buildings.

Frederick and his men halted about the windmill.

Two men produced a crowbar and a sledge hammer.

Do you see what they are doing? They are going to pack blasting powder into that hole.

Terrified, the animals waited. Then there was a deafening roar.

The windmill had ceased to exist!

At this sight the animals' courage returned to them. They charged.

It was a savage, bitter battle. A cow, three sheep and two geese were killed and nearly everyone without injury was wounded.

The men did not go **unscathed**. Three of them had their heads broken by Boxer's hoofs, another was **gored** by a cow's horn. When the dogs of Napoleon's bodyguard appeared, Frederick shouted to his men to get out and the next moment the enemy was running for dear life.

sallied forth – went out bravely
unscathed – without injury
gored – stabbed, pierced

They had won, but they were weary and bleeding. The windmill was gone. Even the foundations were partly destroyed. As they approached the farm, Squealer came towards them and the animals heard the booming of a gun.

What is that gun firing for?

To celebrate our victory.

What victory? They have destroyed the windmill.

What matter? We will build another. The enemy was in occupation of this ground – and we have won it back again.

Then we have won back what we had before.

That is our victory.

Two whole days were given over to celebrations. There were songs, speeches and a special gift of an apple was bestowed on every animal. Napoleon created a new decoration, the Order of the Green Banner, which he conferred upon himself.

A few days later the pigs found a case of whisky in the cellars of the farmhouse.

That night there came from the farmhouse the sound of loud singing.

- Is Boxer right to be puzzled about the 'victory'?
- Which of Major's instructions do the pigs ignore in the farmhouse?

About this time there occurred a strange incident which hardly anyone was able to understand.

One night there was a loud crash in the yard, and the animals rushed out of their stalls.

At the foot of the wall of the big barn, where the Seven Commandments were written, lay a ladder broken in two.

Squealer was sprawling beside it, and near at hand lay a lantern, a paintbrush and an overturned pot of white paint.

The dogs escorted him back to the farmhouse. Benjamin nodded with a knowing air, and seemed to understand, but would say nothing.

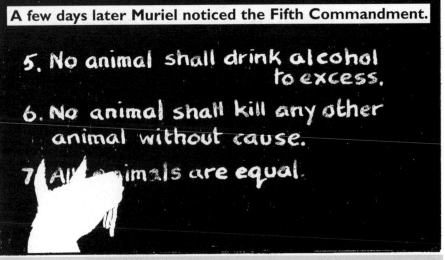

A few days later Muriel noticed the Fifth Commandment.

5. No animal shall drink alcohol to excess.

6. No animal shall kill any other animal without cause.

7. All animals are equal.

- What has happened to the Fifth Commandment?
- What does Benjamin know, and why does he say nothing to the other animals?

They started the rebuilding of the windmill the day after the victory celebrations. Clover and Benjamin urged Boxer to work less hard.

But Boxer would not listen. He had, he said, only one real ambition left – to see the windmill well under way before he reached retirement.

The retirement age had been fixed for horses at twelve. As yet no animal had actually retired. Boxer's twelfth birthday was due the following year.

Meanwhile life was hard. The winter was cold and once again all rations were reduced except for those of the pigs and dogs.

Napoleon commanded that once a week there should be held a **Spontaneous** Demonstration to celebrate the struggles and triumphs of Animal Farm.

LONG LIVE COMRADE NAPOLEON

The animals would leave their work and march round the farm, in military formation, with the pigs leading.

spontaneous – not planned

• Is the Demonstration really 'spontaneous'?

In April Animal Farm was proclaimed a Republic, and it became necessary to elect a President.

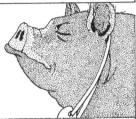

There was only one candidate, Napoleon, who was elected unanimously.

Boxer worked harder than ever.

Indeed all the animals worked like slaves that year.

Late one evening, in the summer, two pigeons came racing in with news.

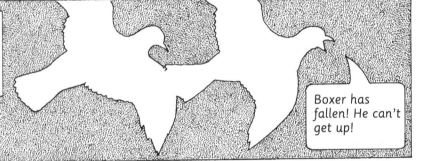

Boxer has fallen! He can't get up!

About half the animals rushed out.

We must get help at once. Run and tell Squealer what has happened.

Squealer said that Comrade Napoleon was already making arrangements to send Boxer to be treated in Willingdon. The veterinary surgeon could treat Boxer's case more satisfactorily than could be done on the farm.

Boxer managed to limp back to his stall.

Clover lay in his stall and talked to him, while Benjamin kept the flies off him.

However, Benjamin and Clover could only be with Boxer after working hours, and it was in the middle of the day when the van came to take him away. The animals were all at work weeding turnips under the supervision of a pig, when they were astonished to see Benjamin come galloping from the direction of the farm buildings, braying at the top of his voice. It was the first time that they had ever seen Benjamin excited – indeed, it was the first time that anyone had ever seen him gallop. 'Quick, quick!' he shouted. 'Come at once! They're taking Boxer away!' Without waiting for orders from the pig, the animals broke off work and raced back to the farm buildings. Sure enough, there in the yard was a large closed van, drawn by two horses, with lettering on its side and a sly-looking man in a low-crowned bowler hat sitting on the driver's seat. And Boxer's stall was empty.

The animals crowded round the van. 'Good-bye, Boxer!' they chorused, 'good-bye!'

'Fools! Fools!' shouted Benjamin, prancing round them and stamping the earth with his small hoofs. 'Fools! Do you not see what is written on the side of that van?'

That gave the animals pause, and there was a hush. Muriel began to spell out the words. But Benjamin pushed her aside and in the midst of the deadly silence he read: "'Alfred Simmonds, Horse Slaughterer and Glue-Boiler, Willingdon. Dealer in Hides and Bone-Meal. Kennels Supplied." Do you not understand what that means? They are taking Boxer to the knacker's!'

A cry of horror burst from all the animals. At this moment the man on the box whipped up his horses and the van moved out of the yard at a smart trot. All the animals followed, crying out at the tops of their voices. Clover forced her way to the front. The van began to gather speed. Clover tried to stir her stout limbs to a gallop, and achieved a canter. 'Boxer!' she cried. 'Boxer! Boxer! Boxer!' And just at this moment, as though he had heard the uproar outside, Boxer's face, with the white stripe down his nose, appeared at the small window at the back of the van.

'Boxer!' cried Clover in a terrible voice. 'Boxer! Get out! Get out quickly! They are taking you to your death!'

All the animals took up the cry of 'Get out, Boxer, get out!' But the van was already gathering speed and drawing away from them. It was uncertain whether Boxer had understood what Clover had said. But a moment later his face disappeared from the window and there was the sound of a tremendous drumming of hoofs inside the van. He was trying to kick his way out. The time had been when a few kicks from Boxer's hoofs would have smashed the van to matchwood. But alas! his strength had left him; and in a few moments the sound of drumming hoofs grew fainter and died away. In desperation the animals began appealing to the two horses which drew the van to stop. 'Comrades, comrades!' they shouted. 'Don't take your own brother to his death!' But the stupid brutes, too ignorant to realise what was happening, merely set back their ears and quickened their pace. Boxer's face did not reappear at the window. Too late, someone thought of racing ahead and shutting the five-barred gate; but in another moment the van was through it and rapidly disappearing down the road. Boxer was never seen again.

 Think About It

1 Why do you think no animal has yet retired with the agreed pension?

2 Are the 'struggles and triumphs' the real reason for the weekly 'Spontaneous Demonstration'?

3 Look again at page 50. Why does no other animal become a candidate for the Presidency?

4 The election of one leader from only one candidate is not *democracy*, it is *dictatorship*. Look up the definitions of these words.

5 What would Major have thought about the animals working 'like slaves'?

6 How do you feel about what happens to Boxer?

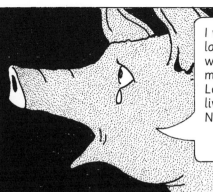

Three days later it was announced that he had died in the hospital, in spite of receiving every attention a horse could have.

I was at his bedside at the very last. And at the end, almost too weak to speak, he whispered in my ear, 'Forward, comrades! Long live Animal Farm! Long live Comrade Napoleon! Napoleon is always right.'

Squealer fell silent for a moment, and his little eyes darted suspicious glances from side to side.

It had come to his knowledge that some of the animals had noticed that the van was marked 'Horse Slaughterer'. The van had been bought by the veterinary surgeon who had not yet painted the old name out.

Napoleon appeared at the meeting on the following Sunday morning. It had not been possible, he said, to bring back their comrade's remains for **interment** on the farm. In a few days' time the pigs intended to hold a memorial banquet in Boxer's honour.

On the day appointed for the banquet a grocer's van delivered a large wooden crate at the farmhouse. That night there was the sound of uproarious singing.

The word went round that from somewhere or other the pigs had acquired the money to buy themselves another case of whisky.

interment – burial

• Where have the pigs got the money from to buy whisky?

Years passed. A time came when there was no one who remembered the old days before the Rebellion, except Clover, Benjamin, Moses and a number of pigs.

The farm had grown richer without making the animals any richer – except for the pigs and dogs.

The animals never lost their sense of honour in being members of Animal Farm. They were still the only farm in England owned and operated by animals.

One day Squealer ordered the sheep to follow him.

He was, he said, teaching them to sing a new song.

After the sheep returned, the terrified neighing of a horse sounded from the yard. It was Clover's voice. The animals rushed into the yard. They saw what Clover had seen.

It was a pig walking on his hind legs. A moment later, came a long file of pigs ...

... and finally Napoleon himself. He carried a whip in his trotter.

Four legs good, two legs better! Four legs good, two legs better!

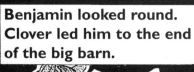

Benjamin looked round. Clover led him to the end of the big barn.

My sight is failing. But that wall looks different.

ALL ANIMALS ARE EQUAL BUT SOME ANIMALS ARE MORE EQUAL THAN OTHERS

The next day the pigs all carried whips. It did not seem strange when the pigs took Mr Jones's clothes out of the wardrobe and put them on.

A week later, neighbouring farmers were shown all over the farm and expressed admiration for everything they saw.

That evening laughter and singing came from the farmhouse. The animals were stricken with curiosity. They tiptoed to the house and peered in at the window.

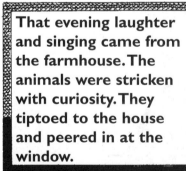

There, round the long table, sat farmers and pigs enjoying a game of cards.

Mr Pilkington, of Foxwood, had stood up, his mug in his hand. In a moment, he said, he would ask the present company to drink a toast. But before doing so, there were a few words that he felt it **incumbent upon him** to say.

his duty

It was a source of great satisfaction to him, he said – and, he was sure, to all others present – to feel that a long period of mistrust and misunderstanding had now come to an end. There had been a time – not that he, or any of the present company, had shared such sentiments – but there had been a time when the respected **proprietors** of Animal Farm had been regarded, he would not say with hostility, but perhaps with a certain measure of misgiving, by their human neighbours. Unfortunate incidents had occurred, mistaken ideas had been current. It had been felt that the existence of a farm owned and operated by pigs was somehow abnormal and was liable to have an unsettling effect in the neighbourhood. Too many farmers had assumed, without due enquiry, that on such a farm a **spirit of licence and indiscipline** would prevail. They had been nervous about the effects upon their own animals, or even upon their human employees. But all such doubts were now **dispelled**. Today he and his friends had visited Animal Farm and inspected every inch of it with their own eyes, and what did they find? Not only the most up-to-date methods, but a discipline and orderliness which should be an example to all farmers everywhere. He believed that he was right in saying that the lower animals on Animal farm did more work and received less food than any animals in the country. Indeed he and his fellow-visitors today had observed many features which they intended to introduce on their own farms immediately.

owners

lawlessness

cleared away

He would end his remarks, he said, by emphasising once again the friendly feelings that **subsisted**, and ought to subsist, between Animal Farm and its neighbours. Between pigs and human beings there was not, and there need not be, any clash of interest whatever. Their struggles and their difficulties were one. Was not the labour problem the same everywhere? Here it became apparent that Mr Pilkington was about to spring some carefully prepared witticism on the company, but for a moment he was too overcome by amusement to be able to utter it. After much choking, during

existed

which his various chins turned purple, he managed to get it out:
'If you have your lower animals to contend with,' he said, 'we
have our lower classes!' This **bon mot** set the table in a roar, and
Mr Pilkington once again congratulated the pigs on the low
rations, the long working hours and the general absence of
pampering which he had observed on Animal Farm.

joke/witty saying

 Think About It

1 Do you think the animals still have reason to be proud of belonging to Animal
Farm?

2 Look again at what Major told the animals (on page 7). Why is Clover 'terrified' by
pigs walking on their hind legs?

3 What had Mr Pilkington been worried about when the animals took over the farm?

4 Why is he no longer worried?

5 Make a list of the ways Napoleon gradually makes himself more powerful and
'important' on the farm. (Look at things like his decorations and titles.)

6 Which animals receive the 'Animal Hero' decoration in the story? Do you think any
of the animals are heroic?

Gentlemen, I give you a toast: to the prosperity of Animal Farm!

Napoleon said he, too, was happy that the period of mis-understanding was at an end.

Gentlemen, I will give you the same toast but in a different form: to the prosperity of the Manor Farm!

There was the same hearty cheering as before.

As the animals outside gazed at the scene, it seemed that some strange thing was happening. What was it that had altered in the faces of the pigs? What was it that seemed to be melting and changing? Then, the applause having come to an end, the company took up their cards and continued the game and the animals crept silently away.

But they had not gone twenty yards when they stopped. An uproar of voices was coming from the farmhouse. They rushed back. A violent quarrel was in progress. Napoleon and Mr Pilkington had each played an ace of spades **simultaneously.** Voices were shouting in anger, and they were all alike.

No question now, what had happened to the faces of the pigs.

The creatures outside looked from pig to man, and from man to pig, and from pig to man again; but already it was impossible to say which was which.

simultaneously – at the same time

● Is there now anything at all left of Major's dream about the future for the animals?